FAVORITE BASKETBALL TEAMS

Boston Celtics

BY K. C. KELLEY

The Child's World®

THE CHILD'S WORLD®
1980 Lookout Drive • Mankato, MN 56003-1705
800-599-READ • www.childsworld.com

ACKNOWLEDGMENTS
The Child's World®: Mary Berendes, Publishing Director
Shoreline Publishing Group, LLC:
  James Buckley, Jr., Production Director
The Design Lab: Kathleen Petelinsek, Design;
  Gregory Lindholm, Page Production

PHOTOS
Cover and interior photos: AP/Wide World

Published in the United States of America.
LIBRARY OF CONGRESS
CATALOGING-IN-PUBLICATION DATA
Kelley, K. C.
  Boston Celtics / by K.C. Kelley.
    p. cm. — (Favorite basketball teams)
  Includes bibliographical references and index.
  ISBN 978-1-60253-305-9 (library bound : alk. paper)
  1. Boston Celtics (Basketball team)—Juvenile literature.
  2. Basketball—Massachusetts—Boston—Juvenile literature.
  I. Title. II. Series.
  GV885.52.B67K45 2009
  796.323'640974461—dc22   2009009786

Table of Contents

Go, Celtics!

Fans of the Boston Celtics expect to end each season one way—at the top! The Celtics have won more NBA championships than any other team. The team wears famous green-and-white uniforms. Many of the game's greatest stars have worn the Celtics' shamrock **logo**. Let's take a look at the great Celtics basketball team!

5

Three happy Celtics celebrate the 2008 NBA championship.

Championship banners hang above the Celtics' home court.

Who Are the Celtics?

The Boston Celtics play in the National Basketball Association (NBA). They are one of 30 teams in the NBA. The NBA includes the Eastern Conference and the Western Conference. The Celtics play in the Atlantic Division of the Eastern Conference. The winner of the Eastern Conference plays the winner of the Western Conference in the **NBA Finals.** The Celtics have been the NBA champions 17 times. No other team has done that well!

Where They Came From

The Boston Celtics are one of the NBA's earliest teams. The Celtics started playing in the Basketball Association of America (BAA) in 1946. That league joined with another in 1949 to form the NBA. From the start, the Celtics were one of the best teams. They made the **playoffs** every year from 1951 through 1969. They won an amazing 11 NBA championships in that time!

The Celtics won their first championship in 1957.

The Celtics and the Lakers have often played big games!

Who They Play

The Celtics play 82 games each season. That's a lot of basketball! They play every other NBA team at least once each season. They play teams in their division and conference more often. Since the 1960s, the Celtics have had a big **rivalry** with the Los Angeles Lakers. Those two teams have often battled in the NBA Finals.

Where They Play

The Celtics play their home games at TD Banknorth Garden. This large indoor arena holds 19,600 people. The team moved into this home in 1995. Before that, they played in Boston Garden. This was one of the most famous places in basketball. Fans loved the old place. Many of the Celtics' biggest games were played in the "old" Garden.

13

Celtics fans support their team at their home court.

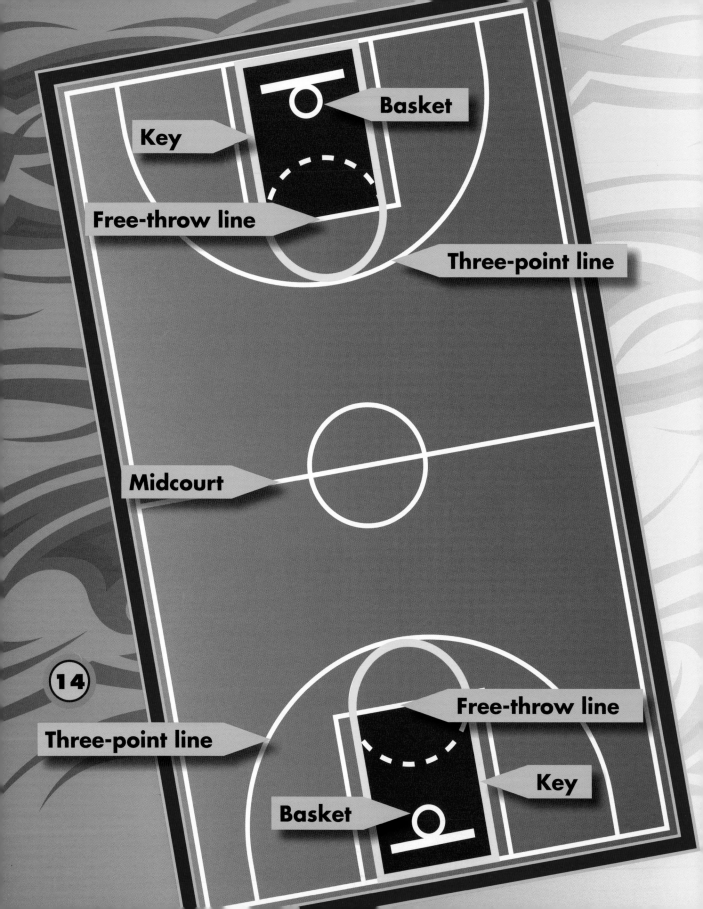

Basket

Key

Free-throw line

Three-point line

Midcourt

14

Three-point line

Free-throw line

Key

Basket

The Basketball Court

Basketball is played on a court made of wood. An NBA court is 94 feet (29 m) long. A painted line shows the middle of the court. Other lines lay out the free-throw area. The space below each basket is known as the "key." The baskets at each end are 10 feet (3 m) off the ground. The metal rims of the baskets stick out over the court. Nylon nets hang from the rims.

Big Days!

The Boston Celtics have had many great moments in their long history. Here are three of the greatest:

1957: The Celtics won their first NBA championship. It was the start of an amazing run of titles.

1966: **Center** Bill Russell became the first African-American head coach in NBA history. He led the team to two more NBA titles.

2008: The Celtics' "Big Three" led the team back to the top. The team won their first NBA title since 1986.

17

Bill Russell and coach "Red" Auerbach were a winning team.

In 1997, the Celtics had a tough time holding on to the basketball!

Tough Days!

The Celtics can't win all their games. Some games or seasons don't turn out well. The players keep trying to play their best, though! Here are some of the toughest seasons in Celtics history:

1985: Though they had one of their best teams ever, the Celtics lost to the Los Angeles Lakers in the NBA Finals.

1997: The Celtics had their worst season ever. They won only 15 games!

2007: The Celtics had one of their worst seasons. They won only 24 games. The next year, however, they were the champs again!

Meet the Fans

Celtics fans love basketball . . . and the Celtics! They are never afraid to yell at the other teams, too. Celtics fans wear the green and white of their heroes. Sometimes they paint their faces with shamrocks! The Celtics play in the state of Massachusetts, in the northeastern United States. Fans in other nearby states root for the Celtics, too!

21

Celtics fans celebrate at a parade after the team's 2008 NBA title.

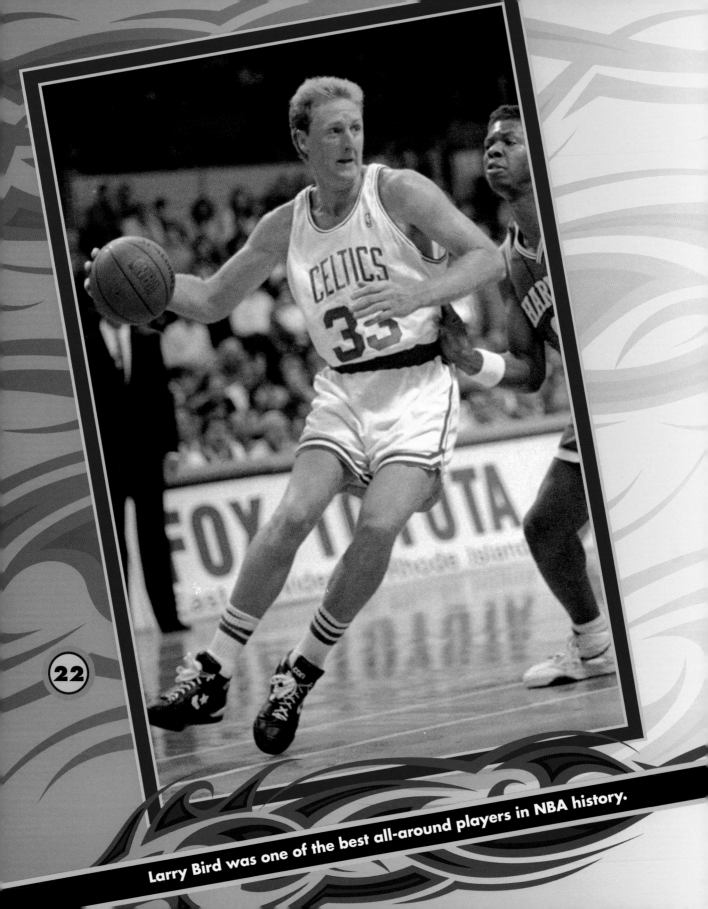

22

Larry Bird was one of the best all-around players in NBA history.

Heroes Then...

The Celtics have had more superstar players than any other team. Here are just a few of them. **Guard** Bob Cousy was an amazing passer and dribbler in the 1950s and early 1960s. Center Bill Russell was the sport's best **rebounder**. **Forward** and guard John Havlicek was a solid **defender** as well as a top scorer. Guard K. C. Jones ran the Celtics' **offense** after Bob Cousy left. In the 1980s, forward Larry Bird came along. He could hit shots from just about anywhere. His passes amazed fans and players. He was probably the best Celtics player ever.

Heroes Now...

Paul Pierce joined the Celtics in 1998. Since then, he has joined the ranks of the NBA's best players. He scores often and also plays tight defense. He was the best player on a so-so team. Then, in 2007, he was joined by two other superstars. Kevin Garnett was one of the league's best forwards. Guard Ray Allen has been called one of the best shooters of all time. Together these "Big Three" players led Boston to the NBA championship in 2008. Young guard Rajon Rondo is a future superstar.

Rajon Rondo splits the defense to take a shot at the basket.

Gearing Up

Boston Celtics players wear a uniform and special basketball sneakers. Some wear other pads to protect themselves. Check out this picture of Paul Pierce and Kevin Garnett and learn about what NBA players wear.

The Basketball

NBA basketballs are made of leather. Several pieces are held together with rubber edges. Inside the leather ball is a hollow ball of rubber. This is filled with air. The leather is covered with little bumps called "pebbles." The pebbles help players get a good grip on the ball. The basketball used in the Women's National Basketball Association (WNBA) is slightly smaller than the men's basketball.

Headband

Jersey

Shorts

Knee brace

Socks

Basketball shoes

27

Paul Pierce and Kevin Garnett are wearing the Celtics' classic green.

Sports Stats

Note: All numbers shown are through the 2008–2009 season.

HIGH SCORERS

These players have scored the most points for the Celtics.

PLAYER	POINTS
John Havlicek	23,395
Larry Bird	21,791

HELPING HAND

Here are Boston's all-time leaders in **assists**.

PLAYER	ASSISTS
Bob Cousy	6,945
John Havlicek	6,114